— Animal Trackers—
TRACKING ANIMAL
BEHAVIOR

Tom Jackson

CAPSTONE PRESS

a capstone imprint

Fact Finders are published by Capstone Press,
1710 Roe Crest Drive, North Mankato, Minnesota 56003
www.capstonepub.com

Published in 2016 by Capstone Publishers, Ltd.

Library of Congress Cataloging-in-Publication Data
Cataloging-in-publication information is on file with the Library of Congress

ISBN: 978-1-4914-6988-0 (hardcover)
ISBN: 978-1-4914-6998-9 (paperback)
ISBN: 978-1-4914-7008-4 (eBook PDF)

For Brown Bear Books Ltd:
Text: Tom Jackson
Designer: Lynne Lennon
Picture Researcher: Clare Newman
Design Manager: Keith Davis
Editorial Director: Lindsey Lowe
Children's Publisher: Anne O'Daly
Production Director: Alastair Gourlay
Picture Manager: Sophie Mortimer

Photo Credits
Front cover: Suzi Esterhas/Minden Pictures/FLPA
1, Jonas Gratzer/Lightrocket/Getty Images; 4, James Michael Dorsey/Shutterstock; 5t, Paulsly/Shutterstock; 5b, AndreAnita/
Shutterstock; 6, Filipe Frazao/Shutterstock; 7, Heiko Kiera/Shutterstock; 8, Czesznak Zsolt/Shutterstock; 9t, visceralimage/
Shutterstock; 9b, Dave Pusey/Shutterstock; 10, Annetje/Shutterstock; 11t, Zoonar/Thinkstock; 11b, Pavel L Photo and Video/
Shutterstock; 12, Wild Wonders Europe/Widstr/Nature PL; 13t, Alta Oosthuizen/Shutterstock; 13b, Ammit/iStock/Thinkstock;
14, Ewan Chesser/Shutterstock; 15t, Jonathan Blair/Corbis; 15b, Jonas Gratzer/Lightrocket/Getty Images; 16, Wild Wonders
Europe/Widstr/Nature PL; 17, Koo/Shutterstock; 18, Jonas Gratzer/Lightrocket/Getty Images; 19, Wikipedia; 20, Greg
Marshall/National Geographic Creative; 21, Netfalls - Remy Musser/Shutterstock; 22t, Michael Nichols/National Geographic
Society/Corbis; 22b, Sean Nel/Dreamstime; 23t, Noam Wind/Shutterstock; 24, Pascal Goetgheluck/SPL; 25, Steve Winter/
National Geographic Creative; 26c, Ralph White/Corbis; 26b, Tanja Rosso/Dreamstime; 27t, JoeBreuer/Shutterstock; 28, Sam
Ogden/SPL; 29, PA Images.
t=top, c=center, b=bottom, l=left, r=right

Printed in China

TABLE OF CONTENTS

WHY WE TRACK ANIMAL BEHAVIOR

Biologists are scientists. They study how animals live. To understand animals, biologists study behavior in the wild. Sometimes they use technology to help them see behaviors that would otherwise be hidden from view.

TYPES OF BEHAVIOR

Animals live in many different ways, but they are all trying to do the same kinds of things. These things include finding food, finding mates, and producing young. All animals also need to keep themselves and their young safe from attack by other animals.

This gray whale is "spyhopping." While **migrating**, the whale pokes its head out of the water. It can see land in the distance, and that helps it find its way.

A male and female lion are fighting. Animals fight over food, mates, and **territory**.

Scientists call these activities animal behavior. Biologists study how different species of animal do these things.

NATURAL CONDITIONS

Animals change their behavior depending on events. For example, if a gazelle is grazing and it detects a lion, it will stop eating and run away. Animals usually change their behaviors when they see humans too. This makes it hard for scientists to be sure they are watching natural behaviors. Technology is used to help scientists track animal behavior without being spotted.

HIDDEN BEHAVIOR

Technology can also be used to record animal behavior when scientists are not there. It can show what animals are doing in places humans cannot go, such as in burrows under the ground or in the deep oceans. From studying behaviors, scientists can understand how animals survive.

These two crowned cranes are performing a courtship ritual. Their behavior creates a bond between them. The cranes will mate every year to produce chicks.

MAKING OBSERVATIONS

The easiest way to study animal behavior is to simply watch animals in the wild. Biologists might spend hours outside watching what the animals do. Scientists also use binoculars and cameras so they can observe behaviors in detail.

CHANGING CONDITIONS

An animal's behavior changes throughout the day and night. Biologists have to observe behavior to understand animals properly. A species' behavior may also change with the seasons. For example, many animals only breed at a particular time of year.

A bird-watcher uses binoculars to look at birds flying over a wetland. Watching animals at a distance helps create a picture of their natural behaviors.

USING SCIENCE

Biologists can often figure out behavior by watching and describing what an animal does. They can learn about **courtship rituals**, which are the behaviors male and female animals perform before they mate. However, scientists must not assume they know what an animal's behavior means without testing their idea scientifically. People used to think that all male bullfrogs croak to attract mates. This changed when scientists noticed that some bullfrogs stay silent. These silent bullfrogs mate with the females that come looking for the croaking males.

OBSERVATION TECHNIQUES

Scientists observe animal behavior with the naked eye while sitting quietly among the animals. They also watch from a distance using a telescope or binoculars. Observations can also be made using cameras that take photographs and videos of behaviors. Cameras can be set up to do this automatically without the researcher being there.

A baby python hatches from its egg. By observing this behavior scientists know that the snake cuts its way out with an eggtooth. This is a pointed horn on the snout that falls off as soon as the head is out of the egg.

HIDING OUT

Getting a good look at animals behaving naturally in the wild is not easy. Most animals are shy and will try to keep away from humans. Scientists have developed ways of staying out of sight.

TAKING COVER

Many animals are camouflaged. This means their fur or skin is patterned to help them blend in with their surroundings. The camouflage makes it harder to see the animals. Wildlife experts copy this idea.

Wildlife experts watch animals from inside well-camouflaged hides. Even the big lenses of their cameras are disguised.

When observing animals, scientists do not wear brightly colored clothes. Instead, they wear clothes that blend in with their surroundings. In some cases scientists dress in full camouflage gear like soldiers wear. To hide completely, scientists sit inside camouflaged shelters, or hides. An animal does not see the person or people inside.

A wildlife researcher is wearing clothes that keep him well-hidden among the dry grass.

OTHER SENSES

Wild animals use their senses of smell and hearing to detect danger. Scientists must be very quiet. Even the slightest sound can scare animals away. Scientists also use the wind to stay hidden. They choose a hiding place where the wind direction will blow their **odor** away from animals, not toward them. If an animal detects the smell of humans it will run away.

A night-vision camera makes it possible to see a leopard drinking at a watering hole at night.

WOW!

Nocturnal animals use the cover of darkness to stay hidden. Night-vision equipment makes it easier for researchers to watch them. This equipment works by picking up the heat given off by the animals' bodies. Human eyes cannot see heat, but the night-vision equipment converts the heat into an image that can be seen.

PICTURES AND VIDEOS

Cameras are useful tools for tracking animal behavior. Many animal behaviors happen too fast for scientists to see them clearly. Looking at videos and photographs allows scientists to study what happens in much more detail.

TOO MUCH, TOO FAST

The behavior of animals that live in groups is complicated. Different animals in the group do different things, and they all do them at the same time. To understand the behavior, scientists study photographs or **slow-motion** video.

For example, a school of fish appears to change direction at the same time. It is almost as if the school was one single animal.

This diver is using an underwater camera. The bright light held above the camera makes it easier to see animals in the dark water.

However, video footage shows that fish on the outside of the school try to swim into the middle. The fish in the middle are too crowded and swim out. The result is the fish always stay in a tight ball, even when the group changes direction.

HIDDEN DETAILS

Cameras can also show how small animals behave. The camera can magnify the animals. Magnified photographs show scientists how bugs feed, hunt, and breed.

A close-up view shows a crab spider attacking a bee landing on a flower.

TECHNOLOGY: Crane camera

A crane camera is a simple system for showing researchers large groups of animals. The camera is raised high above the ground on the arm of a crane. A wire connects the camera to scientists on the ground. They can see what the camera sees from high above the animals.

Vulture watchpoints

Vultures are nature's garbage disposal units. The big birds eat what is left of dead animals. Wildlife lovers use hides to watch the birds in action.

Scientists and wildlife lovers take advantage of vulture behavior to get a good look at the birds. They build hidden watchpoints and then lure the birds to them with food.

Soaring in the sky

Vultures are **scavengers**. They eat the bodies of dead animals. The birds look for animals that have died from old age, or they eat the remains of a meal left by a predator. To find food, vultures soar high above the ground. From this height they can see and smell bodies lying on the ground. The birds then circle down to rip off chunks of meat with their tough, hooked beaks. In dry areas and mountains, where vultures are common, it is normal to see the birds in the sky. However, to watch them on the ground is more difficult. That is why scientists build watchpoints.

Watchpoint

A vulture watchpoint is a high-tech hide. It has mirrored windows. The people inside can see out, but the animals outside cannot see in. The experts inside poke their camera lenses out through curtains under the windows.

Feeding behavior

Scientists use watchpoints to observe vulture behavior. This includes finding out which body parts the birds eat and how they interact with other scavengers, such as **jackals**.

Bearded vulture

This African vulture eats bones. It carries a big bone in its claws high into the air. The bird then drops the bone on rocks below. The bone smashes into chunks that are small enough to swallow.

King vulture

This species from Central and South America is one of the largest vultures in the world. Its wings are 6.6 feet (2 m) wide. It soars over mountains, grasslands, and rain forest looking for food.

Hilltop watchpoints are used to watch the vultures in the air or resting on cliffs.

Vultures soar on currents of warm air that rise up from the ground.

Fresh meat and bones are placed in front of the hide to attract birds.

The ground watchpoint is accessed by a tunnel so the birds are not disturbed.

REMOTE SENSING

Scientists cannot watch everything an animal does. Instead, researchers use technology to track animals 24 hours a day. This type of technology is called **remote** sensing.

SEE IT ALL

Animals have a wide range of behaviors. They may only exhibit some of them once a day or even once a year. Scientists are not able to watch all the time. Remote sensing enables scientists to observe every moment of an animal's behavior.

This elephant has a radio tracker attached to a collar around its neck. The tracker shows scientists where the elephant and her herd go day and night.

TECHNOLOGY: Re using radar

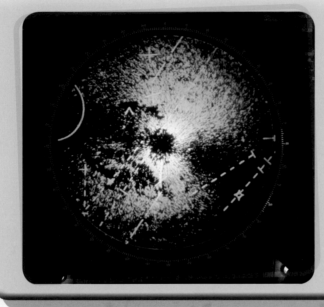

Radar technology was designed for tracking aircraft. It is also used by weather **satellites** to scan for rain. The same radar systems can be used to track animals. This radar scan shows a flock of 2 million birds flying near an airport in the state of South Carolina. Scientists are investigating what made all these birds group together.

TRACKING MOVEMENTS

Trackers are one form of remote sensing technology. These are small devices fitted to animals. They send out signals that tell scientists where the animal is. Trackers help researchers figure out what an animal does at different times of the day. For example, trackers show when an animal is drinking or feeding and where it goes to have a rest.

KEEPING WATCH

Remote sensing equipment is also used to take pictures and video of animals in the wild. This technology is sometimes called a camera trap. It does not trap the animal itself but takes a picture of it. Camera traps are used to study animals that are very rare or difficult to find in their natural **habitat**.

A scientist fits a **trail camera** to a rain forest tree. He will then leave the area so he does not scare away the animals.

15

WEBCAMS

A webcam is a camera that is connected to the Internet. Any photographs or video taken by the camera are sent to a website. Webcams are a good way of watching how animals behave in nests and dens.

A webcam records the behavior of a whiskered tern as it sits on its nest on marshland. This bird lives in Europe, Asia, and Africa.

INTERNET VIDEO

A wildlife webcam uses the same kind of camera as a cellphone or computer screen. However, a webcam is left outside for a long time and needs a tough, waterproof case. Video is sent through the Internet using the same kind of system as videophone programs.

The camera is operated by remote control. It may be turned off at night when it is too dark to take video. Where there is no electricity supply, the camera equipment is powered by batteries or a small **solar panel**. The camera is connected to the Internet by a cable or by a **wireless** link.

ONE LOCATION

Webcams are best for watching nests, dens, and other places where animals return every day (or night). The cameras give a close-up view of the animals resting in the den. If it is breeding season, scientists also watch the animals raising young.

(JOIN IN)

Watching wildlife

There are many wildlife webcams you can watch on the web. Some show live video of animals, while others show examples of interesting behavior. Search online for wildlife webcams. Try these organizations first:

The Wildlife Trusts
Explore.org

There are webcams for eagles and other birds of prey, burrowing animals like badgers, and even for bears.

These badgers are leaving their den, or sett, at dusk. "Settcams" show how the badgers behave as they spend the day underground.

FACT: Some wildlife webcams are on the top of skyscrapers. Falcons nest on tall buildings.

VIDEO TRAPS

Video traps are used to record the behaviors of animals that range over wide areas. These cameras often record very rare behaviors that scientists have never observed.

HEAT SENSOR

The cameras used in video traps do not take pictures all the time. To save battery power they only switch on when an animal moves in front of them. Each camera is fitted with a heat-sensitive detector. When the camera detects the body heat of an animal, it starts filming a video.

Scientists watch a rare Sumatran tiger captured on video by cameras set up in the rain forest.

RARE BEHAVIOR

Video traps allow scientists to watch the behavior of shy animals. Animals, such as tigers and giant pandas, are cautious. Anything unusual stops them from behaving naturally. Video traps have been used to watch both species. Video has also shown that when pandas meet each other they roar to scare each other away. If that does not work, the pandas fight, biting and slashing each other with their claws. The fighting is so violent that the pandas knock down young trees. Video traps show where tigers go when they are resting during the day—they hunt at night. Videos have also shown female tigers playing with their cubs. Few scientists have ever seen this behavior in the wild.

A self-portrait taken by a crested black macaque.

WOW!

In 2011, a wildlife photographer on the island of Sulawesi in Indonesia was taking pictures of crested black macaques, a rare type of monkey. One of the monkeys picked up a camera and started to take pictures—even grinning at the lens.

This monkey species is in danger of **extinction**. There are just 6,000 left in the wild.

CRITTERCAM

A penguin fitted with a crittercam is sliding into a hole in the ice. The camera gives the penguin's view of its hunt for fish to eat.

One of the best ways to understand how an animal behaves is to attach a camera to it. This special camera is nicknamed a "crittercam." Crittercam videos show scientists what an animal is seeing.

BODY CAMERA

Crittercams are designed to not bother the animals wearing them. They can only be fitted to animals large enough to carry one without the camera changing their natural behavior. Crittercams are often placed on the backs of swimming animals, such as sea turtles and sharks.

Crittercams give a close-up view of the behavior of dangerous animals, such as alligators and crocodiles.

The camera does not weigh very much in water, so it does not create problems for the animal. Smaller, lighter cameras have been developed. These can be fitted to land animals, such as lions.

TAKING VIDEO

Crittercams are attached in a number of ways. A shark's camera is clamped to its fin. A penguin or seal is fitted with a special harness. A dolphin or whale has one attached with strong suckers that stick to the animal's smooth skin.

The first crittercams had small batteries and could only take a few minutes of video. To watch the video, scientists had to catch the animal and remove the camera. The latest cameras are designed to detach by remote control. Scientists collect the cameras and download the video.

JOIN IN

Crittercams online

The amazing videos from crittercams are available online. Search online for this organization and look for the links to the crittercam videos:

National Geographic

There are videos of alligators, penguins, sea lions, whales, bull sharks, lions, sea turtles, and even a tree kangaroo. Many of the videos show the animals hunting prey.

21

Lion Hunt

Crittercams and night-vision equipment have allowed scientists to study a lion hunt in more detail than ever before.

Lions are the only cats that work together to hunt prey. A group of lions is called a pride. Prides hunt at night. Researchers use the latest night-vision technology to watch how they do it.

Hunting ground

Most lions live in the grasslands of Africa. They share this habitat with **antelopes.** For safety, antelopes live in herds. They eat grasses and leaves. They are very fast runners and can outrun a lion. Antelopes are the lions' main food. To catch one the lions have to work as a team.

Researchers record lion hunts with a crittercam around a **lioness'** neck. However, scientists normally use special night-vision equipment to see how all the lions behave during hunts.

Night Vision

Researchers stay out of sight when watching lions. They use red lights to help them see in the dark. Lions cannot see that color very well. However, lions can see clearly at night. Their eyes have a mirror-like layer. This reflects the dim light back into the eye so it has enough light to see.

In for the kill

The lionesses form the hunting team. The single male lion in the pride sits and watches with the cubs. The lionesses stay **downwind** of the antelope herd. That means the wind is blowing their smell away from their prey, so the prey cannot smell them. The pride stays out of sight until the lionesses are ready to launch an attack.

2
Some lionesses creep around behind the herd. They jump out and scare the antelopes.

1
Lionesses approach a herd of antelopes from downwind.

3
The herd runs away from the lionesses.

4
One lionesses waits for the herd to get close and grabs one of them.

TRACKING
WITH ROBOTS

Robots help scientists study animal behavior in two ways. First, robots are programmed to copy an animal behavior so scientists can study it. Second, robots can operate in places that are too dangerous for humans.

COPYING BEHAVIOR

Robots are being used to study ants. These insects live in **colonies** containing thousands of animals. Working together, the ants in a colony can do many things. For example, ant colonies build nests, find food, and carry building materials and young over long distances.

A real ant meets a robot ant. The robot is designed to copy the way real ants explore an area.

Tiny robots are used to figure out how ants behave. The robot is designed to move like an ant. It goes in a straight line until it cannot go any further. It then changes direction and goes forward again. Scientists release many robots at the same time. They find that even these simple robots spread out and fill the whole area—just like real ants.

A young tiger investigates a camera robot sent by scientists to take pictures of its behavior.

DANGEROUS PLACES

Robots are sent to places that humans cannot reach. They can be sent to investigate caves, ice-covered seas, and deep water. Robots are all controlled by a human driver. The driver can see what the robot is doing on a computer screen.

FACT: BigDog, a four-legged robot, can run, climb hills, and even throw objects.

ROV Submersibles

Humans cannot visit the animals on the deep seafloor. Robots and other machines are sent instead.

Most of the world's seafloor is more than 1 mile (1.6 km) under the sea's surface. At that depth the weight of all the water above is enough to squash a human body flat. Most of the exploration is done by robots.

Underwater

A submarine is a craft that carries people underwater. Submarines that can go all the way to the deep seafloor are very expensive. Scientists use ROV **submersibles** instead. ROV stands for Remotely Operated underwater Vehicle.

ROVs can reach the deepest parts of the ocean. The ROV is connected to the surface by a long cable. The cable carries electrical power for the engines and steering commands from a human controller. It is always dark on the seafloor. ROVs are fitted with bright lights and cameras so the controller can see and study any animals the ROV might find.

underwater robots

ROVs can be as big as a car or small enough for a person to pick up. They have at least two engines, or thrusters. ROVs are steered by making one thruster push harder than the others.

research ship

While aboard special ships scientists research the oceans. They spend months at sea gathering information. These scientists are called oceanographers. They study ocean life, the weather, and the motion of the water.

This ROV is in two parts. The lower one drops to the seafloor.

Several probes collect samples from the water and the sandy seafloor. Information is sent back to shore by satellite.

Depth sensors show the crew the shape of the seafloor.

Studying the seafloor

The research ship takes many measurements and samples from the water and the seafloor. The ROV sends back pictures and can even capture animals to study. ROVs have detected many new forms of life living in the deepest parts of the ocean.

THE FUTURE

There are many things scientists do not know about animal behavior. In the future scientists will use robots that work like real animals to figure out why animals do the things they do. Drone aircraft will also watch behavior in the wild.

ROBOT ANIMALS

Robot **engineers** often copy animal bodies when they design robots. A robot moves like an animal and senses objects using the same systems. That means a robot can be used for investigating animal behaviors in the laboratory.

Robot tests in the future could tell scientists how much an animal thinks about what it is doing. The robot is programmed to follow simple rules. Scientists will run tests to see how well the robot performs tasks, such as moving around a maze.

RoboPike is a robot fish that can swim by itself. This version is remote controlled. Scientists are developing a robot that can find its way around by itself.

Scientists want to know if the robot does these things in the same way that animals would do them in the wild. If the robot does not behave like a natural animal, that shows scientists that their programmed rules do not match the way an animal makes its decisions. That could mean that animals are taking more things into account before making their next movement. However, if the robot does behave like a wild animal, it might show that animals do not need to think much at all. Even complicated animal behaviors, such as finding food and mates or getting away from predators, only require the animal to perform a few automatic actions.

A park ranger launches a small drone aircraft to track tigers. In the future drones could be used to keep an eye on all kinds of wildlife.

AUTOMATIC AIRCRAFT

Drones are another kind of robot. They are uncrewed aircraft. They may become a useful tool in tracking behavior. In the future drones could stay in the air for many days. They will carry powerful cameras that could watch wildlife closely. Drone research will show how the behavior of one animal can affect the behaviors of others over a wide area.

GLOSSARY

antelopes hoofed animals that have horns

colonies large groups of animals that live and work together

courtship ritual a complex dance-like behavior used by animals to attract mates

downwind to be located in a place when wind is blowing toward you; animals cannot smell things that are downwind

engineers people who use the latest scientific knowledge to build machines

extinction when a species has died out

habitat the places where animals or plants live and grow

jackals small dogs that live in Africa and Asia; jackals live in large packs and mostly eat the remains of dead animals

lioness a female lion

migrating making a regular journey to find food, to find mates, or to raise young

nocturnal to be active at night

odor a smell

radar a technology that bounces radio waves off objects and picks up any echoes that come back; the system is used to detect large objects that are too far away to see with the naked eye

remote when something is a long distance away from anything else

satellite object that orbits (moves around) another larger one; planets are satellites of the Sun, and machines launched in orbit are also known as satellites

scavengers animals that eat the remains of dead animals

slow-motion when real-life action is slowed down so the fast motion can be seen in detail

solar panel technology that generates electricity from sunlight

submersible a submarine that does not have a human crew

territory in terms of biology this is a region controlled by an animal; the animal finds all its food in the territory and tries to stop other members of its species from living there

trail camera a tough camera that is designed to work outside in all weathers

wireless an Internet connection that uses radio waves instead of wires

READ MORE

Animal Behavior Building Blocks of Science. Chicago: World Book, 2014.

Coupe, Robert. *Predators and Prey: Battle for Survival* Discovery Education: Animals. New York: PowerKids Press, 2015.

Harvey, Derek. *Animal Antics: The Funny Things Animals Do.* New York: DK Publishing, 2014.

Rake, Jody Sullivan. *Garbage Gorgers of the Animal World* Disgusting Creature Diets. North Mankato, Minn: Capstone Press, 2015.

Silvey, Anita. *Untamed: The Wild Life of Jane Goodall.* Washington, D.C.: National Geographic, 2015.

Spilsbury, Louise. *Survival of the Fittest: Extreme Adaptations* Extreme Biology. New York: Gareth Stevens Publishing, 2015.

Taylor, Saranne. *Animal Homes* Young Architect. New York: Crabtree Publishing, 2015.

INTERNET SITES

FactHound offers a safe, fun way to find Internet sites related to this book. All of the sites on FactHound have been researched by our staff.

Here's all you do:

Visit www.facthound.com

Type in this code: 9781491469880

Super-cool stuff!

Check out projects, games and lots more at
www.capstonekids.com

INDEX